Natural Disasters

with Dan Quake,
natural disasters expert

Bill McGuire

KINGFISHER

Kingfisher Publications Plc
New Penderel House
283–288 High Holborn
London WC1V 7HZ
www.kingfisherpub.com

First published by Kingfisher Publications Plc 2007
2 4 6 8 10 9 7 5 3 1
1TR/0307/SNPTHAI/SCHOY(SCHOY)/157MA/C

Copyright © Kingfisher Publications Plc 2007

A CIP catalogue record for this book is available from the British Library.

ISBN 978 0 7534 1420 0

Senior editor: Simon Holland
Senior designers: Peter Clayman, Carol Ann Davis
Picture research manager: Cee Weston-Baker
DTP co-ordinator: Catherine Hibbert
Senior production controller: Lindsey Scott

Printed in Thailand

Contents

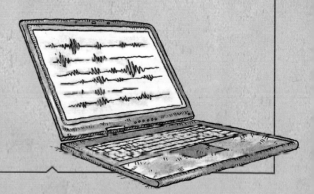

Meet your guide

My name is Dan Quake, and I am an expert on the subject of natural disasters. My job is to try and predict when and where the next natural disaster will strike, and make sure that everyone is prepared. One day I might be in Japan watching a volcano blow its top. The next day I might be helping to dam flood waters in Bangladesh.

"Nature can be dangerous. Weather centres help by sending out severe weather warnings."

Satellite view of Hurricane Katrina hitting the coast of the USA

a volcano in Hawaii spewing
out a fountain of lava

Lightning blasting
a city in the USA

Some natural disasters, such as volcanic
eruptions, earthquakes, tsunamis and
landslides, are caused by the violent
forces beneath our feet. Others, such as
storms, floods, wildfires and droughts,
are caused by our turbulent climate.

flooding in New
Orleans, USA, caused
by Hurricane Katrina

Jigsaw planet

Our world is like a giant, ball-shaped jigsaw puzzle. The outer layer is broken up into huge rocky plates, which sit on a layer of hot, melting rock. The plates creep across the surface of the planet, jerking, jolting and colliding with one another like bumper cars. Where two plates scrape past one another, a weakness in the Earth is formed, called a fault.

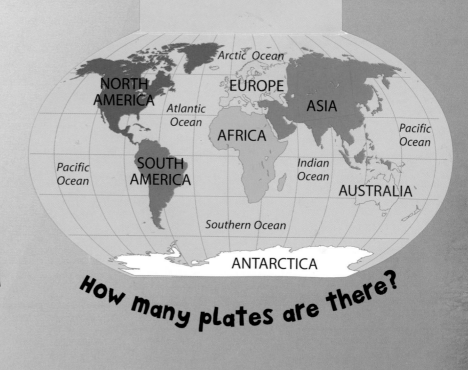

Arctic Ocean

NORTH AMERICA

EUROPE

ASIA

Atlantic Ocean

AFRICA

Pacific Ocean

Pacific Ocean

SOUTH AMERICA

Indian Ocean

AUSTRALIA

Southern Ocean

ANTARCTICA

San Andreas fault Line in the USA

How many plates are there?

Earthquakes occur along the fault lines in the Earth's surface. Where the plates collide or move apart, volcanoes erupt, and geysers and hot springs gurgle up.

a geyser exploding in Iceland

"Sulphur gases bubble up where two of the plates split apart. Pooh! It smells like rotten eggs!"

shake, rattle and roll

An earthquake happens when two huge masses of rock jerk violently past one another. This takes place along faults, the lines of weakness in the Earth's surface. Every year there are more than one million earthquakes, but only about 150 of them are big enough to cause serious damage. The greatest earthquakes can shake entire cities to the ground.

"Along a fault, earthquakes often occur at regular intervals, so we know roughly when the next one is due... but not exactly."

seismometer in the ground

buildings collapse

roads and railways are broken up

surface rupture – cracks in the ground above the fault

earthquake waves – these cause the ground to shake violently

epicentre – the point directly above the earthquake

fault – a fracture in the Earth's crust where earthquakes happen

focus – the point where the earthquake starts

Chinese rescue workers searching for survivors

seismometer reading, showing earthquake shockwaves

Scientists detect and study earthquakes using a seismometer. This sensitive instrument measures the size and strength of an earthquake's waves.

Walls of water

Tsunamis (said 'su-naa-mees') are gigantic walls of water, sometimes taller than a house. They are dangerous because they flood onto land. Most tsunamis form when earthquakes happen under the sea, forcing the seabed up. This disturbs the water above, causing huge waves. Tsunamis can also be caused by erupting volcanoes, giant landslides, or even by asteroids or comets crashing into the sea.

"Often, the sea retreats before a tsunami arrives. If you see this, find higher ground or head inland immediately!"

How do tsunamis happen?

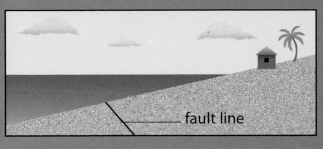

1. There is an active fault line beneath the sea.

fault line

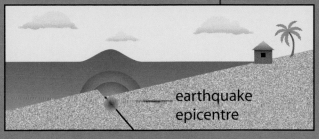

2. An earthquake on the fault line forces the seabed up, and waves head towards the land.

earthquake epicentre

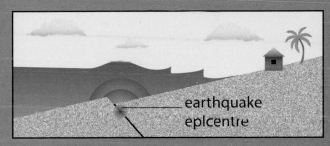

3. The waves get taller as they near the land and the sea draws back in front of them.

earthquake epicentre

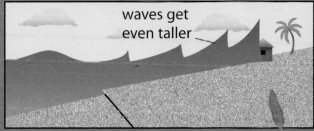

4. The waves hit the shore with enormous force and flood far inland.

waves get even taller

TSUNAMI

EARLY WARNING SYSTEMS

Very volcanic eruptions

A red volcano erupts (throws out) runny lava. The lava forms spectacular fountains or flows across the ground, burying farmland, setting fire to forests and knocking down buildings. At a grey volcano, the lava is much stickier and full of gas. Grey eruptions are far more violent.

"Volcanoes are violent and spectacular. They are our planet's way of losing heat and keeping cool."

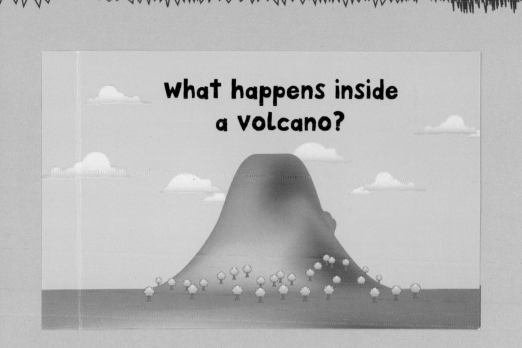

What happens inside a volcano?

A grey volcano throws out enough ash to bury whole towns. Its eruption sends a deadly pyroclastic flow (hot lava and gas) hurtling down the slopes, destroying all in its path.

grey volcano in Montserrat, Caribbean

pyroclastic flow

studying volcanoes

All volcanoes get restless before they erupt. Volcanologists, scientists who study volcanoes, can spot the warning signs. Small earthquakes happen as lava breaks through rock to get to the surface. The volcano also bulges as new lava pushes upwards. Scientists measure this swelling using data from satellites circling the Earth. They also study the lava and gases coming out of a volcano to see if an eruption is on its way.

Lava flowing from a volcano in Hawaii, USA

"Volcanoes are my speciality. Studying them is dangerous, but we have to get close if we are to learn more about them."

collecting a chunk of magma from the lava flow for study

How do we know when a volcano is about to erupt?

Dangerously dry weather

When the weather has been dry for a long time, the result is a drought. In some countries, the drought may not last long, but there may be a ban on using hosepipes and public warnings about saving water. In other countries, periods of drought can have much more lasting and damaging effects.

baked earth around a shrinking reservoir in Australia

crops that have failed due to low rainfall in Africa

In parts of Africa and India, where the weather is normally hot and dry, long periods without rainfall are far more serious. They often lead to the failure of crops and a severe shortage of food and water.

"Water is vital for life. If there is not enough, crops will fail, animals will die and people will starve."

Spreading like... wildfire

Wildfires can destroy huge areas of forest or grassland in just a few days. They often start when there is very hot, dry weather and strong winds. Wildfires can spread faster than a human being can run. Many thousands of wildfires occur every year, and the biggest ones destroy thousands of homes.

a forest fire-break in New Zealand

Wildfires can be slowed or stopped by chopping down trees to form fire-breaks, or by spraying them from the air with water or special chemicals.

Can you see wildfires from space?

fire-fighting plane dropping water _____

"Pets and wild animals often get trapped and killed by wildfires. Some lucky ones are saved by rescue workers."

Water, water... everywhere

Rainwater finds its way into rivers, running over ground or soaking through the ground. But if rain falls too quickly, the ground cannot soak it all up and it may pour into rivers in large amounts. The rivers then swell, burst their banks and flood. If a big storm strikes the coast it can push the sea onto the land, causing even more flooding.

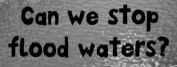

Can we stop flood waters?

people trapped on
a roof after flooding
in the Rio Grande river
valley in Texas, USA

Every year,
millions of
homes are
damaged or
destroyed, and
thousands of people
are killed, by floods.

Chasing cyclones

Tropical cyclones, such as hurricanes and typhoons, are huge storms that form above the warm seas of the tropics. Hurricane-force winds can travel as fast as a sports car. If they strike the coasts, they can cause a huge amount of damage. Tornadoes, also known as twisters, are the most violent of storms. Fortunately, they are much smaller than cyclones.

"Chasing tornadoes is a good way to learn more about them. But it is also scary, as we cannot predict exactly where the twister will go next!"

a storm-chasing vehicle in the USA

an anemometer measures wind speed and direction

Hurricane winds bring down trees and blow away homes. They also bring torrential rains and floods, and massive sea surges that batter coastlines.

heavy rain in New Orleans, USA, during Hurricane Katrina

What happens inside a tornado?

Wacky weather

Sometimes, the weather goes wild without warning. Hailstones as big as tennis balls can crash down, denting cars, smashing roofs and even killing people. Blizzards can bring enough snow overnight to bury an entire town. Freezing rain can turn roads into ice rinks and bring traffic chaos.

car stuck in ice, in Massachusetts, USA

barriers

avalanche

Many ski resorts and mountain villages are protected by barriers that help to trap the snow. Sometimes, when it has been snowing heavily, explosives are used to prevent too much snow collecting on the slopes.

Hothouse Earth

Motor vehicles, factories and fuel-burning power stations pump gases into the atmosphere. These gases act as a blanket, changing the climate and making our planet warmer. People can help the planet by recycling their waste, saving energy and using less fuel.

buildings using lots of electrical energy in New York City, USA

Climate change is causing the ice to melt in the Arctic and Antarctic. This threatens the animals that live in the polar regions.

polar bears in the Arctic

"We need to start using motor vehicles a lot less. Cycling and walking are much better for our planet."

a busy road in the city of Bangalore, India

Glossary

atmosphere The layer of gases that surrounds our planet. It provides the oxygen that living things need to survive.

climate The average weather of a town, city or country over a long period of time.

endangered A plant or animal whose numbers are small and that may disappear altogether.

geyser A fountain of boiling water and steam that is driven by volcanic heat.

hot spring A hot, bubbling stream coming out of the ground in an area of volcanic activity.

landslide A mass of rock or soil that slides down a slope due to an earthquake or very heavy rain.

lava Melted rock that is erupted (thrown out) at a volcano and flows across the land surface.

magma Molten rock produced in the Earth and erupted at the surface through volcanoes.

molten rock Rock that has been heated up so much it melts and becomes a sticky liquid.

pollution Unwanted chemicals or other materials in the air, water or soil that cause damage or make people ill.

recycling Collecting used materials, such as glass, paper, plastic and tins, to make new goods and products.

reservoir An artificial lake made by blocking a river with a dam made of earth, rock or concrete.

satellite A spacecraft that circles the Earth and sends information or pictures back to us.

sulphur A yellow substance that comes from magma. It forms on the surface or gets carried up into the atmosphere.

Index

Acknowledgements

The publisher would like to thank the following for permission to reproduce their material. Every care has been taken to trace copyright holders. However, if there have been unintentional omissions or failure to trace copyright holders, we apologize and will, if informed, endeavour to make corrections in any future edition.

Key: *b* = bottom, *c* = centre, *l* = left, *r* = right, *t* = top

Pages 4–5 Jason Reed/Reuters/Corbis; 4*c* NASA; 5*tl* Pacific Stock/Photolibrary; 5*tr* Warren Faidley/Photolibrary; 6*l* Tom Bean/Corbis; 7*tl* Ifa-Bilderteam/Photolibrary; 7*b* Animals, Animals/Earth Scene/Photolibrary; 9*c* China Foto Press/Getty Images; 9*bl* Bill McGuire; 10–11 AFP/Getty Images; 12 Science Faction/Getty Images; 13 Bill McGuire; 14–15 Roger Ressmeyer/Corbis; 14*(flap)* Roger Ressmeyer/Corbis; 15*r* Roger Ressmeyer/Corbis; 15*bl* Carlos Munoz-Yague/Eurelios/Science Photo Library; 15*bc* Roger Ressmeyer/Corbis; 15*br* Ron Howard/Corbis; 16–17 Photolibrary.Com (Australia); 16*b* Photolibrary.Com (Australia); 17*tl* Sven Torfinn/Panos Pictures; 18–19 David Grey/Reuters/Corbis; 18 Paul A. Souders/Corbis; 19*tl* Bryce Duffy/Getty Images; 19*tr* Armando Arorizo/epa/Corbis; 19*(flap)* NASA/Science Photo Library; 20–21 H. David Seawell/Corbis; 22–23 A. T. Willett/Getty Images; 22*b* Sygma/Corbis; 23*t* Irwin Thompson/Dallas Morning News/Corbis; 24 AFP/Getty Images; 24*br* Empics/Associated Press; 25 AFP/Getty Images; 25*(flap)* Jim Reed/Corbis; 26 blickwinkel/Alamy; 28–29 Corbis; 28*c* Owaki-Kulla/Corbis; 29*tr* Index Stock Imagery/Photolibrary; 29*c* Simon Reddy/Alamy.

The publisher would like to thank the following illustrators:
Sebastian Quigley 9, 21, 23, 26–27;
Lyn Stone (Dan Quake and incidentals throughout);
Peter Winfield 6, 11, 13, 25.